# THE LIBRARY OF CONGRESS

## An Architectural Alphabet

# THE LIBRARY OF CONGRESS

# An Architectural Alphabet

Library of Congress, Washington, D.C.
in association with
Scala Publishers Ltd

© The Library of Congress 2000, 2011

This softcover edition first published
in 2011 by
Scala Publishers Ltd
Northburgh House
10 Northburgh Street
London EC1V 0AT, UK
www.scalapublishers.com

In association with
The Library of Congress

ISBN: 978-1-85759-673-1

Library of Congress
Cataloging-in-Publication Data

The Library of Congress:
    an architectural alphabet /
    The Library of Congress.
        p. cm. – (Scala Publishers cata-
        log ; no. A518)
        Prepared by the Library of
    Congress Publishing Office.
        ISBN 978-1-85759-673-1
        1. Library of Congress Thomas
    Jefferson Building (Washington,
    D.C.) 2. Library architecture–
    Washington (D.C.) 3. National
    libraries–Washington (D.C.)
    4. Washington (D.C.)–Buildings,
    structures, etc. 5. English language–
    Alphabet. I. Title: Architectural
    alphabet. II. Library of Congress
    Publishing Office. III. Series
    Z733.U6.I54 2000
    727'.82573–dc21          99–050105
                                   CIP

Printed in China
10 9 8 7 6 5 4 3 2 1

First published in 2000 in hardcover
by Pomegranate

Prepared by the Publishing Office,
Library of Congress
The Madison Building, LM 602
Washington, D.C. 20540–4980

Director of Publishing:
    W. Ralph Eubanks
Author and picture editor:
    Blaine Marshall
Editor: Margaret E. Wagner
Assistants: Clarke Allen
    and Heather Burke

Consultants: Henry Hope Reed,
president, Classical America, and
author, *The New York Public Library:
Its Architecture and Decoration*;
C. Ford Peatross, curator, Center for
American Architecture, Design and
Engineering Project, Prints and
Photographs Division, Library of
Congress.

Rare Book and Special Collections
Division: Mark Diminunation, chief;
Gerald R. Wager, head of the Reading
Room; Clark W. Evans, reference
specialist; Tracy L. Arcaro, Cynthia D.
Earman, Majid Majd, and Walter
Walden, reference assistants.
Photographic Section: Yousef El Amin
and James R. Higgins Jr. Serial and
Government Publications Division:
Robert R. Shields Jr.

Project director: Diane Maddex
Designer: Robert L. Wiser
Editorial assistants: Gretchen Smith
    Mui and Carol Kim

Page 2: The United States Capitol seen
through a window in the Great Hall's
North Corridor; above the window is a
quotation from Confucius.

Page 5: The Thomas Jefferson Building of
the Library of Congress, whose rich architectural motifs are shown in this book.

Page 64: A circular pendentive painting
by Edward Holslag in the Librarian's
Room, picturing a young reader and the
motto "Reading, the delight of the soul."

Typeset in Diotima, Nofret, and Smaragd,
all designed by Gudrun Zapf-Von Hesse.

**LIBRARY OF
CONGRESS**

# FOREWORD

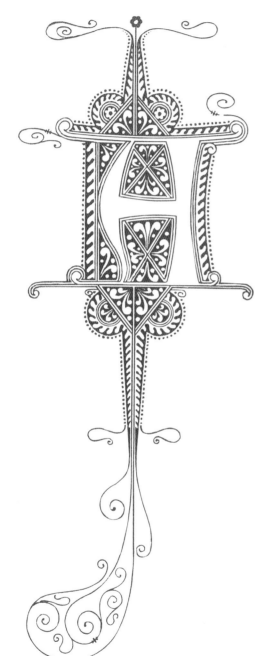

"Architecture presents man," said Frank Lloyd Wright, "literature tells you about him, painting will picture him to you." All of these arts combine in the original Library of Congress building in Washington, D.C., opened in 1897. Now named for Thomas Jefferson, whose personal library became the seed of the Library's world-renowned collections, the Thomas Jefferson Building is a testament to knowledge and creativity and a monument of America's cultural and intellectual heritage. Graced by an ornate facade and an elaborately decorated interior, the building (first known as the Congressional Library) is one of the country's great architectural treasures.

A practical structure as well, the Jefferson Building houses the core of the Library's research facilities—the domed Main Reading Room—as well as many special reading rooms, exhibit areas, and an auditorium designed for musical performances. The music of a great American composer is celebrated in the Gershwin Room, the illustrative arts are featured in the Swann Gallery, and, in the lofty, exquisitely decorated Southwest Gallery and Pavilion housing the Library's first permanent exhibition, representative treasures are displayed for the million or more people who visit each year.

Behind the scenes, miles of book stacks house a portion of the Library's holdings, including those reserved for the Rare Book and Special Collections Division. Centered on a handsome second-floor reading room inspired by a room in Philadelphia's Independence Hall, the division's treasures range from Thomas Jefferson's library to modern artists' books and from broadsides, cookbooks, and dime novels to incunabula, Civil War materials, and children's books. Among the literary landmarks here are the volumes that provided the letters for this book's alphabet: rare books published from the fifteenth to the twentieth centuries in many of the printing capitals of Europe and America.

As the Library of Congress looks back on two hundred years of growth and service to Congress and the nation, we also look forward to new adventures in the digital age. Today millions of people around the world have greater access to the Library's collections and services through our World Wide Web pages. A fascinating architectural primer, *The Library of Congress: An Architectural Alphabet* will also serve, I hope, as an invitation to visit us (in person or at http://www.loc.gov) and learn more about the Library and its amazing trove of more than 115 million items.

At the heart of all our efforts stands the Jefferson Building, a heroic structure that is at once celebratory, inspirational, and educational. Few places represent human aspiration in such dramatic fashion. Indeed, a guidebook published the year the building was dedicated called it "a fitting tribute for the great thoughts of generations past, present, and to be."

*James H. Billington*
*The Librarian of Congress*

# INTRODUCTION

The Thomas Jefferson Building of the Library of Congress was the ultimate expression of the optimism and self-confidence of a vigorous young nation, which set out to construct the world's largest library before it was even a hundred years old. Beginning with an architectural competition in 1873, won by John L. Smithmeyer and Paul Pelz, and continuing with its planning and construction over the next quarter century, the Jefferson Building's architects, engineers, and more than fifty painters, sculptors, and decorative artists and artisans worked in unison to create the most elaborately conceived and embellished public building in the United States.

The Italian Renaissance style was chosen to symbolize the rebirth of knowledge and learning characterized by that period of human civilization. The great rotunda is crowned by a torch of learning, and the force and potential of human imagination, understanding, and genius are celebrated throughout the building, on its exterior and interior, on its floors, walls, and ceilings. The three great bronze entrance doorways celebrate the three great revolutions that by the the building's opening in 1897 had taken place in the transmission of human knowledge: speech, writing, and printing. Today there is a new doorway—an electronic one, representing a fourth such revolution—and the Library of Congress is becoming ever more significant as a portal through which information flows out to the entire world.

The Roman goddess Minerva presides over the entire building as the guardian of civilization. In the Great Hall she is represented as the *Minerva of Peace*, whose strength and vigilance have provided a setting in which the pursuit of learning can flourish and the rays of prosperity can disperse the clouds of ignorance, discouragement, and disaster. She holds a scroll listing all the departments of learning, indicative of the universal range of the Library's collections. As the patroness of peace, of the worker's craft, of inventions, and of the arts and sciences, Minerva is well suited for this role. As the goddess of defensive war, she is directly related to the figure of *Freedom Triumphant in War and Peace* that crowns the dome of the United States Capitol nearby.

Created during a period now referred to as the American Renaissance, the Jefferson Building is a lavish illustrated encyclopedia of the rich and varied forms of classical and Renaissance architecture and decoration. Its beauty was achieved by the hundreds of artists, artisans, and laborers who gave so much of themselves for our ongoing edification and joy. As the building passes its centennial and the Library of Congress approaches the bicentennial of its founding as our first cultural institution, the delightful alphabet that follows serves as an invitation to enjoy but a small taste of its many glories. As you progress from A to Z, keep in mind that the Jefferson Building and its embellishments were created not only to delight but also to celebrate our potential, individually and in the family of nations, and to engage our material and human resources toward the further progress of civilization.

*C. Ford Peatross, Curator*
*Center for American Architecture,*
*Design and Engineering Project*
*Prints and Photographs Division*

# ARCH

An arch on the second floor of the Library's Great Hall gives entrance to an alcove and makes an elegant frame for W. B. Van Ingen's semicircular painting *L'Allegro*, or Mirth, which is showcased in a lunette. The setting in the East Corridor near the Visitors' Gallery staircase is surrounded by a forest of columns supporting saucer domes. The decorations on the vaulted ceiling include paintings of seated women representing *Comedy* and *History*, two in a series of eight pendentive figures by Walter W. Shirlaw.

# BALUSTRADE

Howard Sill's 1893 watercolor shows the balustrade, a short series of supports topped by a rail, that crowns two levels of arches in the Main Reading Room. The upper arches open onto a loggia, a roofed open gallery, and the ground-floor arches lead to book alcoves. The great pier at right, behind an engaged column, is made of Italian marble.

## CLOCK

Directly across from the public entrance to the Main Reading Room stands a clock sculpted by John Flanagan. It is a classic example of how clocks are used architecturally to make a statement about time. A winged Father Time, armed with his scythe, seems to leap out into the space of the huge room. He is flanked by female figures and infants, while below on either side of the clock sit two young readers. Directly beneath the clock is a smaller bronze panel entitled *Swift Runners*. The gold-leaf mosaic background of the composition contains the signs of the zodiac, reinforcing the message of passing time.

# DOME

In the center of the Library's dome, a 125-foot hemispherical ceiling over the Main Reading Room, floats a painting by Edwin Blashfield, *Human Understanding Lifting Her Veil*. Attended by two children, the central figure represents the high purpose of the study taking place below. Surrounding this central painting is a large circular collar painting, also by Blashfield, that depicts various civilizations and eras whose contributions aided America's growth and intellectual achievement. Eight ribs intersect the dome and divide it into graduated sections containing elaborately ornamented stucco panels with square coffers and rosettes.

# EGG AND DART

Rows of square coffers punctuate the domed ceiling of the Main Reading Room. In their centers, like boutonnieres, are gilded rosettes, each tucked into a frame of golden egg-and-dart molding: egg shapes alternating with arrows or darts. One of the most popular in classical architecture, this molding can be found throughout the Jefferson Building.

# FOUNTAIN

Roland Hinton Perry's magnificent fountain in front of the main entrance to the Jefferson Building comes to life at night in the play of the basin's light and water. Allegorical figures in bronze inhabit the granite grotto: Neptune, lord of the seas, is enthroned in the center niche, with Tritons blowing conch shells on either side. Neptune is flanked in the two outside niches by sea nymphs, or nereids, astride frantic sea horses. A sea serpent, two frogs, and four turtles complete the fountain's denizens.

# GALLERY

The many windows of the Northwest Gallery admit natural light, which is brilliantly reflected on the inlaid marble floor. This is one of two galleries off the Great Hall on the second floor; the other is located on the building's southwest side. These long, beautiful spaces are used for exhibits, lectures, and receptions. In the tympanum above the doors at the north end of the Northwest Gallery is Gary Melcher's painting *War;* a companion painting on the south end illustrates *Peace*.

## HELIX

At the entrance to the Visitors' Gallery on the second floor of the Great Hall are Corinthian columns whose capitals sport a helix, or volute, at the tip of the acanthus leaves. The particularly deep carving of the capitals suggests frozen waves: they spiral out from the tops of paired columns flanking the gallery staircase.

# INLAY

A pair of smiling cherubs appears in a panel of wood
inlay on the walls of the Thomas Jefferson Congressional
Reading Room in the Southwest Pavilion's ground floor.
These cherubs, depicted in light mahogany that
has been inserted into darker oak, seem to greet the
distinguished users of the room with a wave.

# JAMB

In this richly decorated commemorative arch, the jamb, which is the vertical side of the archway, includes a shaft with a capital and base. This arch celebrates the completion in 1897 of what is known today as the Jefferson Building, the first of the Library's three structures. Above the jambs of the arch are two life-size figures, *The Students*, by Olin Warner. The younger one on the left reads to acquire the experience of the past, while the bearded older man appears absorbed in reflection.

# KEYSTONE

During construction in 1892, the keystone—the wedge-shaped top stone used to close an arch—was lowered snugly into place in the southwest clerestory arch. (A clerestory is the upper part of a wall containing windows.) The Capitol Hill area, before it became crowded with buildings and cars, can be seen in the distance.

# LANTERN

Crowning the Library's dome is a lantern, a circular domed rooftop structure with windows, and above the lantern rises a blazing torch holding a gilded flame. The emblematic Torch of Learning marks the center and apex of the building, 195 feet above the ground.

# MOSAIC

Elihu Vedder's mosaic *Minerva* is the focus of the Great Hall's second floor. Thousands of small pieces of colored glass created the 9-by-15½-foot likeness of Minerva, goddess of war and wisdom. Here she is shown having laid down her shield and helmet to concentrate on civilized pursuits recorded on the scroll she reads. According to the Latin quote at the base of the panel, her monument—the Library building—is built to be more lasting than bronze.

AGRICULTURE
EDUCATION
MECHANICS
COMMERCE
GOVERNMENT
HISTORY
ASTRONOMY
GEOGRAPHY
STATISTICS
ECONOMICS
PAINTING
SCULPTURE
ARCHITECTURE
MUSIC
POETRY
ZOOGRAPHY
GEOLOGY
BOTANY
MEDICINE
PHILOSOPHY
LAW
POLITICS
ARBITRATION
TREATIES
ARMY NAVY
FINANCE
ART OF WAR

NIL INVITA MINERVA QUAE MONUMENTUM
AERE PERENNIUS EXEGIT

# NEWEL

Poised atop the newel, a post at the top or bottom of a flight of stairs, this bronze figure by Philip Martiny in the Great Hall raises a torch topped with a lighted globe as if to greet visitors. She stands on the right side of the lower turning of the Grand Staircase. This leads to opulent second-story galleries framed by double columns that support marble arches. Beside her, under the stair rail, are eight delightfully antic little boys sculpted in marble by Martiny, each dressed to represent an occupation—from a diminutive hunter proudly clutching a rabbit to a serious mechanic with a cogwheel and pair of pliers.

# OVERDOOR

The overdoor for the entrance to the Thomas Jefferson Congressional Reading Room is an exuberantly carved panel in oak by Herbert Adams. The two smiling winged mermaids hold a helmet over a cartouche bearing the monogram "U.S.A." A swag of banded leaves hangs from either side.

# PILASTER

The square pilasters on either side of the South Corridor on the first floor are vertical projecting features of the walls, treated to look like columns. The representation is complete, each having a base, shaft, and capital. These pilasters are located in the Hall of the Greek Heroes, named for the nine painted panels by Walter McEwen that depict well-known episodes in classical myth and literature. The mosaic floors reflect light from overhead lamps suspended from a succession of saucer domes.

# QUOIN

The Library's quoins, or blocks of stone forming the corners of the building, are treated to set the corners apart from the surrounding blocks. Granite from Concord, New Hampshire, was used for the Jefferson Building's exterior walls: rock faced at the basement level, vermiculated ("worm holed") for the first story, and smooth on the second story.

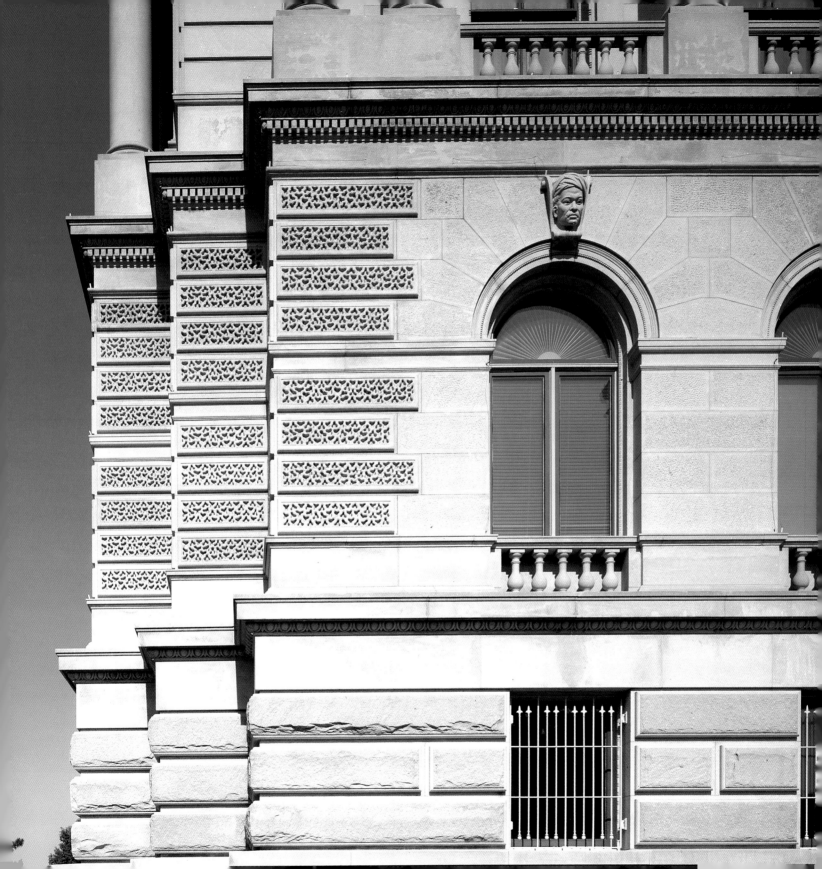

SPRING

# R E L I E F

*Spring*, representing one of the four seasons, is a sculptural relief, or raised work, by Bela Pratt. Located in the Pavilion of the Discoverers on the Library's second floor, the white stucco work depicts a girl sowing seeds, her clothes blown by spring winds. Each of the four pavilions has a different set of the seasonal bas-reliefs. The large medallions are framed by gilded egg-and-dart molding and topped by a banded garland of leaves and other seasonal attributes.

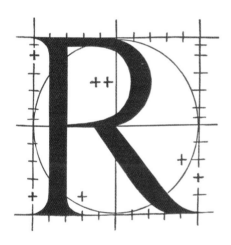

# SPANDREL

The six life-size female figures leaning gracefully in the three entrance arch spandrels, the triangular spaces flanking the upper curve of the arches, represent *Literature* at left, *Science* at center, and *Art* at right. Designed by Bela Pratt, they are carved in granite. In *Literature,* the left figure connotes the productive side of writing and the right figure the contemplative side. In *Science,* the first figure holds a torch of knowledge and the second a celestial globe. In the final pair of spandrels, representing *Art,* the figures of *Sculpture* and *Painting* work on their creations.

## TRIPOD

This stucco tripod, a three-legged vessel with a bowl to hold burning oil, is one of a pair placed on the end walls of the vestibule of the Library's main entrance. Highly decorated with rams' heads, swags, and lions' paws for feet, the tripods serve as sconces for a double row of electric lights and are enlivened by circles of bronze leaves.

# URN

Interspersed among square coffers with gilded rosettes in the dome of the Main Reading Room are urns that form a repeated motif. Along with the urns, which are large vases with a foot, some forty-five other motifs jostle for space on the dome's plasterwork surface, including lions' heads, sea horses, dolphins, cartouches, griffins, shells, storks, caryatids, tridents, eagles, cherubs, and fanciful figures. Adapted from High Renaissance models, this menagerie forms a surprisingly balanced and restrained design.

# VAULT

In the South Corridor is a series of ceiling vaults. Mosaics containing the names of twenty lyric poets enhance and enliven the curved lines of the arches and pendentives. Oliver Walker's paintings in the lunettes, such as *Lyric Poetry* (visible at the end of the corridor), show scenes from poems by Milton, Shakespeare, Keats, Wordsworth, Tennyson, and Emerson.

# WINDOW

A window in the ceiling of the Great Hall filters light through yellow and blue stained glass whose circular, or scale, motif reflects the marble floor below. Elaborately paneled beams, decorated with aluminum leaf, divide the skylight into six identical square windows.

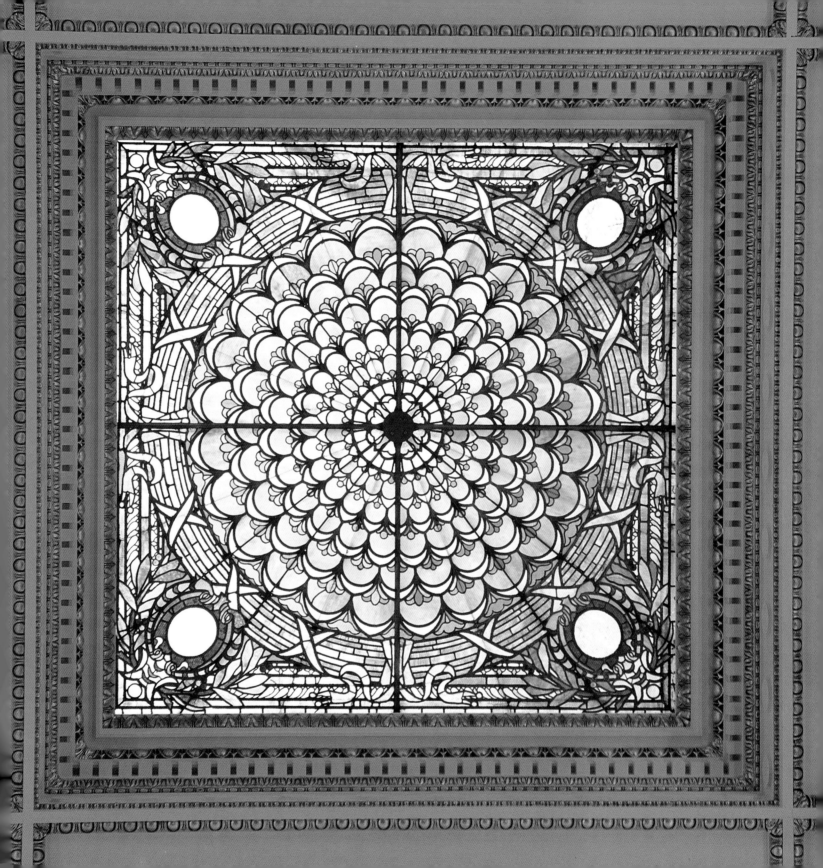

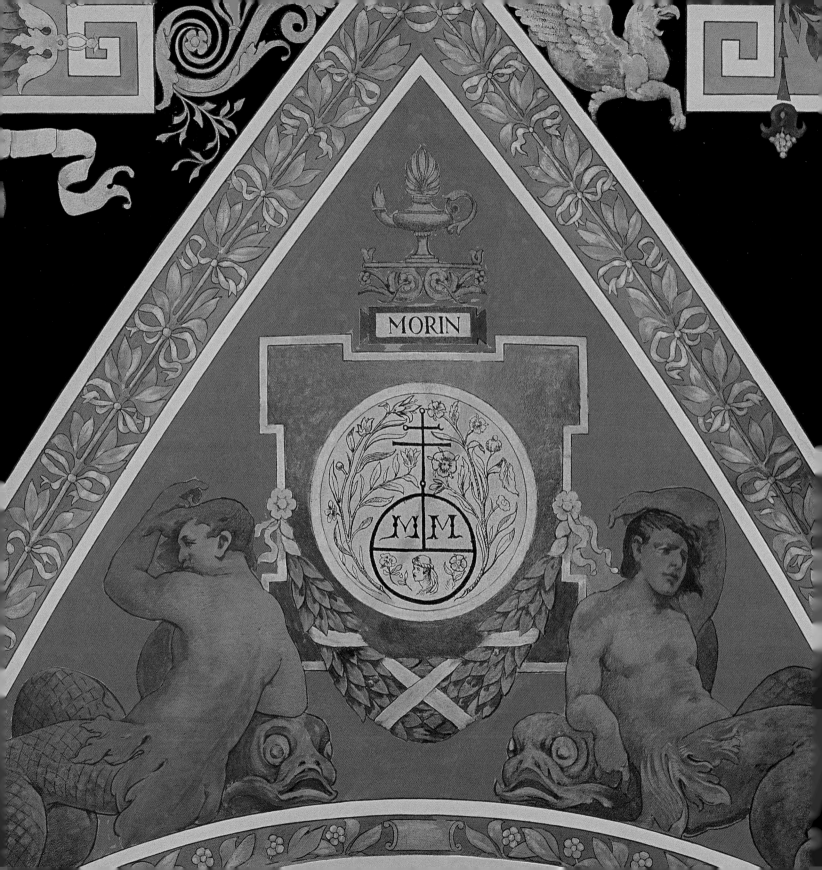

MORIN

# X - MOTIF

On the second floor of the South Corridor, a ribbon-banded X-motif fastens laurel-leaf swags in an arch beneath the mark of Morin, a French printer of the late fifteenth and early sixteenth centuries. Banded X-motifs are commonly used to bundle garlands of bay, laurel, or olive leaves. The walls of all four corridors contain fifty-six printer's marks—engraved devices once used by printers as an informal trademark on the title page of their books.

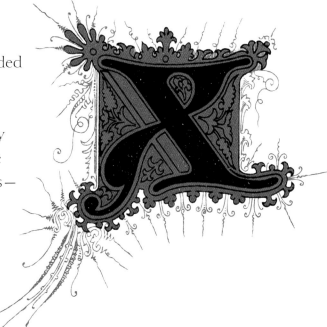

# YOUTH

In a detail from the allegorical lunette *Good Administration,* a youth bends down to drop his ballot into an urn beside a seated woman, whose insignia—the balanced scales of justice—decorates her shield. One in a series of five lunettes on the general subject of government painted by Elihu Vedder, the series appears in the corridor outside the Main Reading Room. Young men and women were often used in classical art to convey the idea of human promise.

# ZIGZAG

The mosaic floor of the Pavilion of the Discoverers includes a dramatic zigzag, or chevron, motif in white, outlined with black, as part of its circular pattern. The four corner pavilions often house exhibitions. Here, under a white-and-gold dome, exhibit cases display Library treasures. The Southwest Gallery can be seen through the open door.

# CREDITS

PHOTOGRAPHS

Architect of the Capitol: V (64055), Y (67308)

Reid Baker: F

Anne Day: cover, case binding, A, C, D, E, G, H, I, N, O, R, page 64

Jim Higgins: page 5, B (LC-C4-1507-color)

Carol Highsmith: endpapers, page 2, J, L, M, P, Q, T, U, W, X, Z

Library of Congress Collections:
K (LC-USZ62-51462), S (LC-USP6-6527A)

LETTERS

Foreword: *Prang's Standard Alphabets*. Boston: L. Prang and Company, 1886.

A: *Brigittine Psalter*. Near Utrecht, Netherlands, ca. 1500. Parchment.
DeRicci no. 114; Faye and Bond no. 86.

B: Gradual. Northern Italy, fifteenth century. Parchment.
DeRicci no. 119; Faye and Bond no. 91.

C: *Prang's Standard Alphabets*. Boston: L. Prang and Company, 1886.

D: Uncataloged manuscript fragment.

E: *Prang's Standard Alphabets*. Boston: L. Prang and Company, 1886.

F: Eike von Repgow, compiler. *Sachenspiegel*. Southern Germany, ca. 1500.
Vellum. Faye and Bond no. 146.

G: *Prang's Standard Alphabets*. Boston: L. Prang and Company, 1886.

H: *Alphabet: International Annual of Letterforms*.
Vol. 1. Birmingham, England: J. Moran, 1964.

I: Geoffrey Chaucer. *The Works of Geoffrey Chaucer.*
Middlesex, England: Kelmscott Press, 1896.

J: *Prang's Standard Alphabets.* Boston: L. Prang and Company, 1886.

K: *Prang's Standard Alphabets.* Boston: L. Prang and Company, 1886.

L: Stanley Morison. *Fra Luca de Pacioli of Borgo S. Sepoleno.*
New York: Grolier Club, 1933.

M: *Prang's Standard Alphabets.* Boston: L. Prang and Company, 1886.

N: Uncataloged manuscript fragment.

O: *Prang's Standard Alphabets.* Boston: L. Prang and Company, 1886.

P: *Woodtype.* New York: Wells and Webb, 1854.

Q: Medieval manuscript. Tours, ca. 1470. Vellum.
DeRicci no. 121; Faye and Bond no. 93.

R: Bruce Rogers. *Champ Rosé.* New Rochelle, New York: Peter Pauper Press, 1933.

S: *Prang's Standard Alphabets.* Boston: L. Prang and Company, 1886.

T: *Alphabet: A Type Miscellany.* Broadside portfolio. 1974.
Reprint, New York: American Printing History Association, 1994.

U: Asa Bullard. *The Pretty Alphabet.* Boston: Phillips and Sampson, 1888.

V: *Prang's Standard Alphabets.* Boston: L. Prang and Company, 1886.

W: *Proef van letteren.* Harlem, Netherlands: Joh. Enschedé en Zonen, 1768.

X: *Prang's Standard Alphabets.* Boston: L. Prang and Company, 1886.

Y: *Kate Greenaway's Alphabet.* London: Routledge, 1885.

Z: Patricia Healy Evans. *An Alphabet Book.* San Francisco: Peregrine Press, 1953.